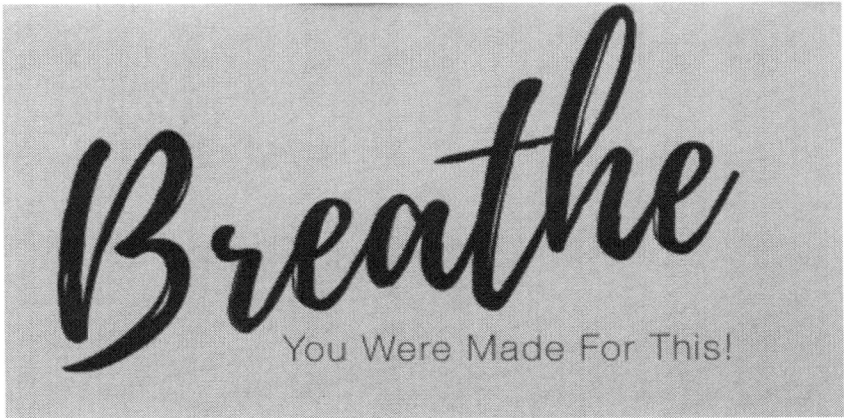

Written By

Women of Compass Christian Church Staff

WEEK 1:
WHO IS GOD?

DAY 1: CREATOR
By Amy Weir

*

Psalm 102:25-26 (NIV)
"Long ago you laid the foundation of the earth and made the heavens with your hands. They will perish, but you remain forever; they will wear out like old clothing. You will change them like a garment and discard them."

My dad's birthday was this week. He is 82 and suffers from advanced Dementia. It's impossibly hard to watch, because my dad was a man of God; strong, smart and kind. He provided for us financially and led us spiritually. In my eyes, he could do anything, and now he struggles to blow out candles on a birthday cake. I know the day is coming when he will not know me, his only daughter, because his mind is slowly deteriorating. His birthday was a sweet time for us to cherish with him, not knowing what next year will look like for him.

In Psalm 102:25, we are reminded that God is the creator of everything. He "laid the foundation of the earth and made the heavens with his hands." God is the author of our days. He made each of us and uniquely placed us in our relative positions in life. He placed us in our family, in our neighborhoods, in our jobs – all as a part of His plan. The same plan that had Noah build an ark, David meet up with Goliath and Jesus rise from the dead. It's all His plan, and as his creations, we are a part of that plan! It's so comforting, in this world that can seem chaotic, that God is in control.

God existed before us. He created every inch of the universe. The universe is changing and wearing down, just like my dad's mind and body...just like my own body.

Psalm 102:26 (NIV)
"They will perish, but You will remain forever"

One thing remains - our steadfast Creator.

"You weren't an accident. You weren't mass produced. You aren't an assembly-line product. You were deliberately planned, specifically gifted, and lovingly positioned on the Earth by the Master Craftsman." – Max Lucado

Nehemiah 9:6 (NIV)
"You alone are the Lord. You made the skies and the heavens and all the stars. You made the earth and the seas and everything in them. You preserve them all, and the angels of heaven worship you."

Daily Focus

Knowing that God is in control, is there something you are struggling with today that you need to give to God to handle?

_____

_____

_____

Write a prayer today using the acronym **PRAY** below:

Praise -

_____

_____

Repent -

_____

_____

Ask -

_____

_____

Yield-

_____

_____

DAY 2: LOVE
By Maureen Hilt

∗

John 4:8 (NIV)
"God is Love and who ever does not Love does not know
God, because God is Love."

John goes even further in scripture and says if we are children of the One whose very nature is love, then we will be like our Father. But it is not automatic or effortless! There is always room for growth.

How simple the love we have for our children as babies and how beautiful to see how they love us back unconditionally. One of the many blessings of having had a special needs daughter, was the gift she had to love others without any conditions.

Having been blessed with three other children in the household as well, many times Brittaney, our special needs daughter, was the one to remind us about loving one another all the time. In Brittaney's mind, she had no filters, no one was different, no one was more special, everyone was loved by Jesus.

I have so many times believed that when God gives us children with special needs, he equips them with more gifts then we know. The physical and health issues special needs children deal with on a day to day basis, is more than enough in life to ask why of God. Yet they never do, they reach out and love life and enjoy simple pleasures every day. They see the world simple and everyone equal. Just like God's commands us to love one another, special needs children do it so naturally.

I received pure joy so many times, while watching Brittaney take on the world, one person at a time. Her joy was contagious and her love for others always came first.

Let us love one another so that when you walk away, your love and Joy remains with them.

Daily Focus

Is there anyone in your life that needs you to show God's love? How can you do that? Be creative.

_____

_____

_____

Write a prayer today using the acronym **PRAY** below:

Praise -

_____

_____

Repent -

_____

_____

Ask -

_____

_____

Yield-

_____

_____

DAY 3: STRENGTH
By Selah Burnett

$*$

Philippians 4:13 (NIV)
"I can do all things through Christ that strengthens me."

Can someone give what they do not have? Christ is capable of giving us strength because He possesses strength. As someone who lost her father as a child, survived a horrific accident, lost family friends to suicide, was a victim of abuse, saw loved ones struggle with Alzheimer's, watched people lose their battle to cancer and held their hand as they passed, and faced anxiety I recognize the importance of strength. Alone, I could not have survived all the hardships that have passed my way.

You see, I recall being 12, after my dad died, and my mother telling me to rely on Christ. I had no hope because I had lost my very best friend. My strength was not enough. Throughout my life, I have not only had to rely on Christ's strength once, but again and again. I had to learn how to rest in the comforting arms of my Lord and Savior. He continually restores my soul, and He empowers and strengthens me to walk in His calling on my life.

Jesus is strong enough to carry your burdens for you, and He will give you the strength to press on. Be confident in this, God loves you. He will carry you when you feel too weak to move.

Prayer for When You Need More Strength:

Father God, Please be with me when I feel weak or inadequate. Remind me of your unfailing love for me and your purpose for my life. May you be glorified through my weakness; make me aware of the moments when I am relying on your strength. Thank you for sacrificing your life for mine. Lord, today, please show me how to minister to others who feel hopeless or weak. In Jesus name, I pray. Amen.

Daily Focus

What areas of your life do you feel weak or inadequate? Ask God today to help you see yourself the way He sees you.

_____

_____

_____

Write a prayer today using the acronym **PRAY** below:

Praise -

_____

_____

Repent -

_____

_____

Ask -

_____

_____

Yield-

_____

_____

DAY 4: PROVIDER
By Anna Watson

✳

John 6:35 (NIV)
"Then Jesus declared, 'I am the Bread of Life. Whoever comes to me will never go hungry and whoever believes in me will never be thirsty."

In John 6, Jesus provides in a miraculous way by using five loaves of bread and two fish from a faithful young boy to feed over 5,000 people. Read that again; marinate on that for a moment. Does it take your breath away when you really think about the impossibility of that? Could you, in your resourcefulness as woman, feed a family of four with a few fries and a chicken nugget? If he can turn a young boy's small lunch into a feast for thousands, then he can certainly provide for us today.

This is beautiful and powerful news. But, it is still not the ultimate point; we are missing the big picture. We find it a few verses earlier. Jesus is having a conversation with those he had just miraculously fed, and they want to know more about him and are comparing him to Moses and his provision of food in the wilderness all those years ago.

John 6:32-33 (MSG)
"Jesus responded, 'The real significance of that Scripture is not that Moses gave you bread from heaven but that my Father is right now offering you bread from heaven, the real bread'."

Here's what we miss: if God can provide for our daily needs (which He absolutely does), how much more does he provide for us in spiritual ways? He gave his life so we could experience salvation. Even now, he gives grace, mercy, and unimaginable peace. He died for us, and he sustains us.

These words hit me in the gut. How often do I doubt that God will provide in some way? How often have I been awake at night thinking about all the things that I need to fix or take care of, just knowing that I had to do it on my own? What about you? How many times have you stopped praying (or maybe never started) because you doubted His provision?

Dear sweet woman, don't hold on to your anxieties any longer. You can trust him with your worries, just as much as you can trust him with your eternity. What things to do you need to relinquish control of today in order to experience his provision?

Daily Focus

What holds you back from trusting God to provide for you?

_____

_____

_____

Write a prayer today using the acronym **PRAY** below:

Praise -

_____

_____

Repent -

_____

_____

Ask -

_____

_____

Yield-

_____

_____

DAY 5: PROTECTOR
By Kelley Carpender

✳

John 10:11 (NIV)
"I am the good shepherd. The good shepherd lays
down his life for his sheep."

Divorce is not something you want to think about let alone do, but after seven long years of praying, scouring scriptures, talking with Christian friends and having heated conversations with God in the car, my marriage ended in a divorce. I had to figure out where to go? How was I going to pay for a place to live? Secure a job? As I stepped out on faith with this decision, it was amazing to see how things fell into place. Jobs were secured (I had 2 that equaled a 40-hour work week), an apartment was found that fit our needs perfectly (my three boys came with me). Don't get me wrong, money was TIGHT! But, bills were paid, and one job went full time and that was a great relief!

During all this upheaval and turmoil, I was praying to not let me make ANY decision without His permission. I had a lot of discussions with God in the car when I was alone. Thank goodness for Bluetooth! Now-a-days it doesn't look strange for someone to be talking to no one in the car! One of the main scriptures that got me through all of this was John 10:11 (NIV).
"I am the good shepherd. The good shepherd lays down his life for the sheep".

Jesus is the good shepherd and can be trusted. He will protect you. By praying and seeking His guidance, He helped smooth the way. Not everything was perfect. It was difficult at times but God protected us through it all. You see, only God knows the perfect plan for me and I wanted to be right smack dab in the middle of it!

Daily Focus

Have you ever thought of God as your protector?
How does this change the way you see Him?

_____

_____

_____

Write a prayer today using the acronym **PRAY** below:

Praise -

_____

_____

Repent -

_____

_____

Ask -

_____

_____

Yield-

_____

_____

DAY 6: SALVATION
By Elisa Copeland

*

John 14:6 (NIV)
Jesus says "I am the Way, the Truth and the Life".

With four kids, a husband, and a dog, it seems like I am always searching for something in my house. The most popular item is my phone charger which goes missing on a daily basis. If you are like our family, we search high and low until we usually find it in plain sight. The most comical item would be my hairspray that my 12 year old son stole from my bathroom every morning of 7th grade. I'm thankful that God isn't hard to find! The way to God is through Jesus.

In John 14:6 Jesus says *"I am the Way, the Truth and the Life"*. Jesus doesn't merely point us in the right direction, He *IS* the direction. If we know Him we know God. So who is Jesus?

Jesus is kind (Luke 8:40-48)

Jesus understands us (Philippians 2:5-8)

Jesus protects us (2 Corinthians 4:8-9)

Jesus loves us (Romans 5:8)

Jesus fights for us (John 8:1)

Jesus stops at nothing to show us just how much He loves us.

I don't know about you, but no one else has ever died for me. What I see through Jesus is a God who is on my side and wants to be close to me. To know Him is to recognize that Jesus died for me and accept His love. Who knew that finding God would be way easier than finding my car keys in a toddler toy bin.

Daily Focus

Which of the descriptions of Jesus do you struggle with believing? Why is it so difficult to believe?

_____

_____

_____

Write a prayer today using the acronym **PRAY** below:

Praise -

_____

_____

Repent -

_____

_____

Ask –

_____

_____

Yield-

_____

_____

DAY 7: CONSISTENT
By Toni Buttner

*

Hebrews 13:8 (NIV)
"God is the same yesterday, today & forever"

Have you ever had a deep yearning in your heart that you prayed God to answer? I have. The days, months, and years go by and you wonder why the Lord hasn't answered. I have often wondered, 'have I not been obedient enough? Doesn't God want the best for me?' Of course He does. Our Heavenly Father delights in giving us good things.

Matthew 7:11 (NIV)
"If you, then, though you are evil, know how to give good gifts to your children, how much more will your Father in Heaven give good gifts to those that ask Him?"

There is no such thing as a perfect, pain-free life. But, you can find peace in the midst of your grief and time of waiting. What do you do when you are waiting for God to provide for you?

You trace God's faithfulness. Beth Moore, Bible study author and speaker, once said, "We often remember what we should forget, and forget what we should remember." How has God answered your prayers and met your needs in the past? Replay those events in your mind and as you do, thank the LORD for what He has done, what He is currently doing, and what He will do for you in the future. God does not change. He is the same yesterday, today and forever!

One of the songs that has encouraged me in my journey is "Do it Again (Live)" by Elevation Worship. Google it today and let it remind your heart that God has accomplished in the past, He is able to do again.

Daily Focus

How has God answered your prayers and met your needs in the past? List those events out on a 3 x 5 card or post-it note. Put it in a place you'll see it, like your bathroom mirror or in your purse.

Write a prayer today using the acronym **PRAY** below:

Praise -

_____

_____

Repent -

_____

_____

Ask -

_____

_____

Yield-

_____

_____

WEEK 2:
WHO DOES GOD SAY YOU ARE?

DAY 1: LOVED
By Kathy Brasher

✻

Romans 5:8 (NLT)
"But God showed his great love for us by sending Christ to die for us while we were still sinners."

Most of us can remember a time as a kid when our parents told us to clean up before dinner or clean our rooms or our cars. The idea that we need to be presentable gets engrained in us as we grow up, and continues to sink its roots deep within us. Some of us spend hours in the morning picking out the perfect outfit, putting on make-up and fixing our hair, or making sure our jewelry is the newest trend.

We work so hard to present ourselves with a certain image, and it often becomes an obsession. Little did we know it doesn't end after high school, college or when we get married. As we get older it sometimes gets worse. We go on vacations, buy a home, or a bigger car and other things that we cannot afford simply to impress others.

We may appear to be put together on the outside, but many of our hearts are a mess. But God doesn't come into our lives and demand we clean ourselves up before we approach him. He loves us when we're messy, then he makes us clean. He proved his love through Jesus giving his life for us on the cross. God doesn't love us because we fix ourselves, he loves us even in our sin, and invites us into Jesus' righteousness.

Daily Focus

Do you struggle with the idea that God requires us to "clean up" before he'll accept us? How has God spoken to you about His love for you even in your sin?

_____

_____

_____

Write a prayer today using the acronym **PRAY** below:

Praise -

_____

_____

Repent -

_____

_____

Ask -

_____

_____

Yield-

_____

_____

DAY 2: CHOSEN
By Robyn Crocker

*

Colossians 3: 12 (NIV)
"Therefore, as God's chosen people, holy and dearly loved,
clothe yourself with compassion, kindness, humility,
gentleness and patience."

I have realized in the past couple years; a lot of the things I do are because I am afraid of rejection. I have a huge fear of letting someone down and being written off. One mistake and I'm being completely rejected, not even by someone in particular, it could be someone off the street. It is a fear that I see creep up in my work, friendships, relationships, everything really.

This has affected my relationship with God immensely. It has created a lot of guilt and shame in my life for past sins that I have committed and sought forgiveness for over and over. Even though I know God forgives, I have an irrational fear He is keeping a tally and at any point, I am done. He will deem me unworthy.

I think a lot of us live this way. We do things not because we want to, but because we fear rejection. We approach our relationship with God, not out of love but out of fear and guilt. Satan has a way of using this to make us believe we are unworthy of the love God as if we will never live up to His expectations.

But you are worthy. You are chosen by God. He chose you, not for the things you have done, or not done, but because you are created in His image. He created you exactly how He wanted. He chose you before you were even born. Over and over again in the Bible, one thing is true. God loves us and He chose us. It's a simple truth we need daily. God has called you His own. He chose you, He loves you. He picked you!

1 Peter 2:9 (NIV)
"You are a chosen people. You are royal priests, a holy nation, God's very own possession."

God wants you, He cherishes you. He loves you.

But this is not the end. Just because we were chosen, doesn't mean we have reached the end. Now we are to live as chosen and holy people. Colossians 3:12 says' "Since God chose you to be the holy people he loves, you must clothe yourselves with tenderhearted mercy, kindness, humility, gentleness, and patience." We are to love each other, just as Christ loves us. These traits should be rampant in how we treat each other.

My prayer is that you live a life in the confidence of being chosen by God and that you live a life worthy of that calling.

Daily Focus

How can you clothe yourself with tenderhearted mercy, kindness, humility, gentleness, and patience?

_____

_____

_____

Use today to ask God to help you live a life with the confidence that God chose you. Write a prayer today using the acronym **PRAY** below:

Praise -

_____

_____

Repent -

_____

_____

Ask -

_____

_____

Yield-

_____

_____

DAY 3: CHILD OF GOD
By Gretchen Griffin

*

1 John 3:1 (NIV)
"See what great love the Father has lavished on us, that we should be called children of God! And that is what we are! The reason the world does not know us is that it did not know him."

When I was growing up, my dad had a nickname for me. As a baby, he called me "Monkey" because I was all over the place, but as years went on it shortened to "Monk". My dad has since passed, but to this day, my brother still calls me "Monk", and I still answer to that.

We all have different names that we answer to in our life. We have our names that our parents gave us at birth, this is the name that the world knows us by, our friends, co-workers, and acquaintances. We have different names for the different roles we play in our lives - wife, sister, best friend, aunt, cousin, the list goes on and on. A very important name for many of us is Mom. We start as "Mommy" when our kids are little, and "Mother" when they become teenagers who are totally annoyed by us!

Some of us take on the many names which negatively affects us – broken, abandoned, divorced, etc. We let it change who we are, we start to believe it is what we are. We let it attach itself to us, hold us back from being what God has called us to be.

Take this to heart, lock it away, and trust in the fact that God created you in His perfect image. God makes no mistakes!

Daily Focus

Repeat this 3 times aloud. Write it out. Claim it!

"I am a child of God, even with all of my earthly flaws. He calls me by name, the name He has for me. My name is child of the one True King, my name is Chosen One, my name is Redeemed."

_____

_____

_____

_____

_____

_____

Write a prayer today using the acronym **PRAY** below:

Praise -

_____

_____

Repent -

_____

_____

Ask -

_____

_____

Yield-

_____

_____

DAY 4: WORK OF ART
By Claire Heath

*

Ephesians 2:10 (NIV)
"For we are God's masterpiece. He has created us anew in Christ Jesus, so we can do the good things he planned for us long ago."

I love to think of God as the potter, the great creator that molds and shapes pieces of clay. It's easy to open the window and see a beautiful sunrise or go to the beach and see the ocean to be reminded of how God is a masterful artist. It's harder to look in the mirror and think the same thing.

I know it's hard for me. When I look into the mirror, I often see someone shadowed by brokenness and sin. I see secrets I've kept to myself, expectations I'll never meet and a dreamer broken by the dreams that never came true. In these moments, I feel like I was knocked off of God's table and shattered on the ground like pieces of broken pottery. What potter would ever be happy with His broken masterpiece?

In the Japanese culture, there's a pottery form called "kintsukuroi". Japanese potters will take broken pieces of pottery and mend it back together with gold or silver. Pieces of handmade art are revered for the care it took to make, its beauty and purpose. But broken, the object is demoted and loses its honor so to speak. Repaired, however, can raise the object to a whole new level of appreciation. The idea is that these pieces are more beautiful for having been broken.

Isn't that why God sent Jesus? God created us and Jesus saves us. Jesus, the Lord of the universe, sacrificed himself so you can be pieced back together with His blood to be a part of His kingdom and to fulfill your purpose as God's greatest masterpiece.

You are more beautiful having been broken. You are found worthy, righteous and desired by God. There is no flaw in you *because* of what Christ did on the cross. Every crack and blemish you believe is on your record has been reversed.

Take a moment today to reflect on the places in your life you feel broken. Ask Jesus to remind you that he's made you whole again and that your worth is not defined by the cracks and the blemishes. You are defined by what He did on the cross that has made you new again so you can do the good things God planned for you since the moment He created you.

Daily Focus

Look up the following scriptures. Write down your thoughts of each one.

Jeremiah 18:1-6

Isaiah 64:8

2 Corinthians 5:17

Hebrews 8:12

Ephesians 2:10

Write a prayer today using the acronym **PRAY** below:

Praise -

_____

_____

Repent -

_____

_____

Ask -

_____

_____

Yield-

_____

_____

DAY 5: VALUABLE
By Barbara Schneider

*

Matthew 6:26 (NIV)
"Look at the birds of the air; they do not sow or reap or store away in barns, and yet your heavenly Father feeds them. Are you not much more valuable than they?"

This scripture is one that I refer to frequently. I am a worrier! My daughters are worriers. We frequently indulge in "what if" scenarios. What if something happens? What if? What if my girls marry the wrong man? What if? What if? What if?

As they were growing up, I frequently would refer to this scripture to calm us. God places such a high value on us! His love for us is above our ability to understand. His plan for redeeming us back to Him, is so that we can have a close relationship with Him. The only way for that to occur was for the supreme sacrifice of Jesus. He gave us his Son, to minister on this earth and show us the way to live. He planned for Jesus to suffer and die for us on the cross; and then rise from the dead – all so that we can have close relationship with Him! That is how much he values you and me!

I believe that daily, and sometimes hourly, we have to remember how much God values us. He knows our troubles and trials that we are going through. He is walking through them with us. Lean on Him to guide you through sickness, financial struggles, job issues, decisions large and small that you need to make. Talk to Him. He loves you and values you above all His creation! He will not fail you! When we worry over our issues, we are disregarding His love for us. You are His most valuable daughter; He will always love you and care for you. You are cherished and valuable.

Daily Focus

What are the "What If's" that you struggle with handing over to God? Why do you think it is difficult to believe that God will take care of you because you are valuable to Him?

_____

_____

_____

_____

_____

Write a prayer today using the acronym **PRAY** below:

Praise -

_____

_____

Repent -

_____

_____

Ask -

_____

_____

Yield-

_____

_____

DAY 6: FORGIVEN
By Anne Milam

✷

Psalm 103:12 (NIV)
"As far as the east is from the west, so far has he removed our transgressions from us."

I love this verse for so many reasons. I love the simplicity of what scripture says, that when we are forgiven. God completely removes our sin, our transgressions and no matter what we do, He won't place them on us again! I love that we see King David's heart in a season when he is able to be grateful for forgiveness because he has wrestled with his own sin. He understands at a core level what it means to have his sin cast so far that he cannot reach it again. I am so grateful to be the recipient of that grace because of my own sin!

But another part of me has a love/hate relationship with this scripture. I know that if God forgives *me* like this...that I am supposed to do the same for others.

And honestly, a lot of times I don't...

want...

to do it...

Really Lord, the person who did *THAT*, I am supposed to forgive them? Like this? But I can't. I just can't. How do you expect me to do this Lord?

Here is where God is so generous with me, with us.

No, we are not all-powerful beings who can cast the hurt done to us completely away in one moment. We may not be able to completely forget. But if we faithfully work day by day to forgive, I believe God will honor us with a forgiveness we never thought we could give.

Often I will decide to forgive someone only to discover in a moment when I least expect it, I am angry and unforgiving of them all over again. This happens over and over. Maybe I had to spend time with this person, or have to deal with the results of their sin against me...again.

It's in these moments I have a choice, wallow in this anger and resentment (and believe me, I have made that choice many, many times), or I can choose to forgive again...and again...and again. Many times I have to keep forgiving over and over. Especially when the effects of the sin against me are long reaching.

Here is how I find I can do what feels impossible on my own. I ask God for help. I ask for the Holy Spirit to fill me and help me in my unforgiveness. When I consistently do that, every time the hurt rises, I find that somehow I can forgive and the angry reaction comes less and less. God is then able to use me and the hurt to glorify Him and to bring me peace.

Daily Focus

Do you ever "remind" God of a sin of which you have already been forgiven?

_____

_____

_____

Write a prayer today using the acronym **PRAY** below:

Praise -

_____

_____

Repent -

_____

_____

Ask -

_____

_____

Yield-

_____

_____

DAY 7: FREE
Written by Alison Williams

✳

Galatians 5:1 (ERV)
"We have freedom now, because Christ made us free. So stand strong. Do not change and go back into the slavery of the law."

When you think of the word FREEDOM, what is the first thing that comes to mind? I think for many, we gravitate towards our constitutional rights, maybe a friend or family member who has, or is currently serving in our armed forces. I come from a long line of amazing veterans in my family, and they have fought hard for the life I lead today.

While I am extremely proud to live in a nation where we value political freedom, I am more encouraged to live in the truth and eternal freedom that comes from following Jesus Christ. *SPIRITUAL FREEDOM* doesn't come from law, it comes from LOVE. *SPIRITUAL FREEDOM* doesn't come from control, but *SURRENDER*. When we give our lives to Christ, we are freed from our guilt, freed from our sins, and even freed from the standards society places upon us.

One of my favorite quotes is from Ronald Reagan:

> "Freedom is never more than one generation away from extinction. We didn't pass it to our children in the bloodstream. It must be fought for, protected, and handed on for them to do the same."

How are you protecting and fighting for your spiritual freedom? By studying HIS word? His word equips us with the ultimate freedom, hope + peace. How are you showing HIS love to others? Because, before all other things, God is love.

Make this day amazing. Go live out the freedom and joy *HE* has given us!

Daily Focus

Read Ephesians 1:7 and John 8:34-36. Write down your thoughts on these two passages.

_____

_____

_____

Write a prayer today using the acronym **PRAY** below:

Praise -

_____

_____

Repent -

_____

_____

Ask -

_____

_____

Yield-

_____

_____

WEEK 3:
RELATING TO GOD

DAY 1: GOD'S WORD
By Karon Arita

✳

Hebrews 4:12 (NIV)
"For the Word of God is living and active. Sharper than any double-edge sword, it penetrates even to dividing soul and spirit, joints and marrow; it judges the thoughts and attitudes of the heart".

The Word of God is alive like the One who spoke it. It is the "discerner" and it produces results. In the Word, we see God and understand how God sees us.

Warren W. Wiersbe said, "The Word exposes our heart and then if we trust God, the Word enables our hearts to obey God and claim His promises."

It has the power to defeat Satan and his lies. God's Word convicts and comforts. It cuts through to truth and freedom. God's Word cuts through **loneliness**.

Deuteronomy 31:8 (NIV)
"The LORD himself goes before you and will be with you; He will never leave you nor forsake you".

It cuts through **insufficiency.**

2 Corinthians 9:8 (NIV)
"And God is able to bless you abundantly, so that in all things at all times, having all that you need, you will abound in every good works."

It cuts through **fear**.

Isaiah 41:10 (NIV)
"So do not fear, for I am with you; do not be dismayed for I am your God. I will strengthen you and help you; I will uphold you with my righteous right hand."

God's Word cuts through **hopelessness**.

Psalm 27:13-14 (NKJV)
"I would have lost heart, unless I had believed that I would see the goodness of the LORD in the land of the living. Wait for the LORD; be of good courage, and He shall strengthen your heart."

Time and time again, when I earnestly seek to hear from God through His Word, He gives me a truth that is vital to continue on walking in obedience to Him. I have come to know that they are not just idle words for me rather they are my life.

Deuteronomy 32:47 (NIV)
"They are not just idle words for you - they are your life. By them you will live long in the land you are crossing the Jordan to possess."

Daily Focus

Have you ever thought of God's word as a living and active way to hear God? How does this change the way you read the Bible?

_____

_____

_____

Write a prayer today using the acronym **PRAY** below:

Praise -

_____

_____

Repent -

_____

_____

Ask -

_____

_____

Yield-

_____

_____

DAY 2: PRAYER
By Kim Post

*

Matthew 6:5-6 (NIV)
"When you pray, you are not to be like the hypocrites;
for they love to stand and pray in the synagogues and
on the street corners so that they may be seen by men.
Truly I say to you, they have their reward in full. But
you, when you pray, go in to your inner room, close
your door and pray to your Father who is in secret,
and your Father who sees what is done in secret will
reward you."

*"God does not give us everything we want, but he does fulfill
his promises....leading us along the best and straightest paths
to himself." Dietrich Bonhoeffer*

I grew up thinking the purpose of prayer was to ask
God to give me what I wanted or thought I needed.
Other than saying Grace before a meal to thank God
for the food, my prayers were more about me than
God. As I matured as a Christian, I began to
understanding the elements of prayer....worship,
confession, thanksgiving, requests...that praying
wasn't just about requesting things of God but also a
way to build a relationship with Him. I think the

more you know about God, the richer and deeper your prayers become.

As I'm getting to know God through studying and applying his Word, I find most scripture has layers of wisdom. For instance, the passage containing the Lord's prayer is perhaps the most well-known passage in the Bible. In it, Jesus gives us an example to follow when we pray. It has praise, adoration, confession, requests for protection, guidance and provision. Did you ever notice in this passage, Jesus says "when you pray" and not "if you pray"? Praying is not a suggestion, but a requirement in order to have a relationship with God. It's the starting point of receiving the gift of salvation (forgiveness of sins and eternity with God), praying to accept the gift and declare your intention to follow Christ.

So after you have prayed and started a relationship with God, what role does prayer play in continuing that relationship? Like any growing, healthy relationship, you need to communicate, and your communication shouldn't just be requests. In the Lord's prayer, Jesus says "Give us today our daily bread." That sounds like a request for food we need to sustain us each day, which we all need, but I think it's even more than that. Jesus also said in John 6:35, "I am the bread of life." When he suggests we pray for daily bread, He is referring to requesting God to provide for our spiritual life each day. Maybe He's suggesting we focus on the Bread of Life we need to sustain us today and allow ourselves to be guided by the Holy Spirit. Since God already knows what we need and want, our prayers full of worship and thanksgiving are really more of a way to rest in God and trust Him with every aspect of our lives.

Daily Focus

Who showed you how to pray? Does understanding prayer as a relationship builder with God change the way that you pray?

_____

_____

_____

Write a prayer today using the acronym **PRAY** below:

Praise -

_____

_____

Repent -

_____

_____

Ask -

_____

_____

Yield-

_____

_____

DAY 3: SIN
Written by Kayla Hurst

✳

Psalm 32:1-5 (NIV)
"Blessed is the one whose transgressions are forgiven, whose sins are covered. Blessed is the one whose sin the Lord does not count against them and in whose spirit is no deceit. When I kept silent, my bones wasted away through my groaning all day long. For day and night your hand was heavy on me; my strength was sapped as in the heat of summer. Then I acknowledged my sin to you and did not cover up my iniquity. I said, 'I confess my transgressions to the Lord.' And you forgave the guilt of my sin."

Why does the Bible ask us to confess our sins? Doesn't He know everything? Why do I have to tell Him what I've done, when He saw me do it to begin with? Some believe that we must confess every single, specific sin so that we can be forgiven by God. If any sin is left unconfessed, we will not be forgiven for that sin. But the Bible is clear that we must be forgiven of all sins or we do not qualify to be with God in Heaven. This is a tragic way to walk through life and it completely empties grace of its power!
You see, because Jesus lived a perfect life. Because He was 100% God and 100% man. Because He conquered sin and death. His sacrifice on the cross was:

Perfect

Complete

Final

So, we're back to the first question: Why does the Bible ask us to confess our sins?

Picture your soul like a candle. When we believe and accept Jesus as our Lord and Savior, when we are baptized, the candle is lit. It's Jesus –by His sacrifice on the cross- who makes our candle burn bright. Now, let's imagine sin as a mason jar. As you sin, the mason jar slowly lowers over the candle. You can still see the candle burning, the flame is still there, and it doesn't seem to make that much of a difference. Sin can seem to have little effect on the outside… for a little while. But as the jar coves the candle more and more, the flame begins to flicker and fade because there's no oxygen.

Sin suffocates our soul. But, when we confess our sins our soul can breathe again! Our relationship with God is reignited every time we come to Him in humility and confess our sins.

"The aim of confession is not to erase consequences, it's to restore joy." – John MacArthur

Daily Focus

What sins in your life do you need to confess before God today?

_____

_____

_____

Write a prayer today using the acronym **PRAY** below:

Praise -

_____

_____

Repent -

_____

_____

Ask -

_____

_____

Yield-

_____

_____

DAY 4: SERVING
By Cara Richardson

＊

2 Corinthians 9:8 (NIV)
"And God is able to bless you abundantly, so that in all things at all times, having all that you need, you will abound in every good work."

Ever since I was a little girl, I have had the gift of gab. My parents would joke that I could talk to a wall and make friends. I have never really met a stranger. I actually remember getting grounded from talking! The people in my life would say that although I seemed shy, the reality was that I just needed to warm up to a situation and then watch out! I would not have thought of this as a "blessing." But God knew what he was doing when he created me this way.

Over time I have learned how to use my "gift of gab" for God. I have learned this is one of my spiritual gifts. We all have these special gifts – hospitality, leadership, compassion for others, etc. The goal is to use these gifts to serve God. When we use the gifts we have been given abundantly *SO THAT* we can do good works. I love connecting with people. It makes my heart happy to meet new people and connect them to Jesus. It is when I use my God-given gifts that I connect to God in an incredible way.

Daily Focus

Do you have a skill (meeting needs of others, talking to strangers, playing a musical instrument, humor, etc.) that you need to leverage for the Kingdom of God? Pray today about the way God created you and where God needs you to serve?

_____

_____

_____

Write a prayer today using the acronym **PRAY** below:

Praise -

_____

_____

Repent -

_____

_____

Ask -

_____

_____

Yield-

_____

_____

DAY 5: SACRIFICIAL GENEROSITY
By Nancy Fitzgerald

*

Psalm 119:35-37 (NLT)
"Make me walk along the path of your commands, for that is where my happiness is found. Give me an eagerness for your laws rather than a love for money! Turn my eyes from worthless things, and give me life through your word."

Growing up in an upper middle class suburb of San Diego, "things" were very important to me. During my adolescent years, these things were clothes, accessories, or whatever made me fit in and be popular. Going to college put things on hold, as I went through the starving student years. But, once I joined the workforce, things became important again. This time, things included my car, my apartment, my friends, the gym I joined, and of course, clothes were still on the list. These things made me look good to others, or that was the goal. I made a pretty good living and had some nice things. So, life was great, as you can imagine. Or was it?

One of the things that wasn't in my life was Jesus. My car did not give me peace when I was dealing with struggles at work. My apartment did not give me strength to stand up to people who were hurting me. My friends did not give me hope for the future. I became a follower of Jesus as an adult after my family left California and moved to Texas. Having

Him in my life has given me a new perspective. He gives me peace when I have struggles. He gives me strength to stand up for what I believe. He gives me hope for my future.

When I take my mind off of things and focus on Jesus, and study God's word, pray, and especially when I listen, God leads me. He reminds me of His promises. His promise of a future helps remind me that because He loves us so much we were worth dying for. His sacrificial love and generosity are what drives us to seek after Him daily. He helps me to be obedient. He teaches me. He gives me insight.

I recently read this quote from an unknown author, "We get attached to temporary things, then wonder why our happiness never lasts." So true. ALL things are temporary. Jesus is not. Following Jesus leads to Eternal Life, and that means much more to me than having the newest designer purse.

Daily Focus

Do you struggle with the love of this world (money, status, cars, careers, etc.)? Why is it important to be reminded of God's sacrificial generosity as it pertains to our worldly desires?

_____

_____

_____

Write a prayer today using the acronym **PRAY** below:

Praise -

_____

_____

Repent -

_____

_____

Ask -

_____

_____

Yield-

_____

_____

DAY 6: TELLING YOUR STORY
By Courtney Pembleton

✳

2 Corinthians 3:2-5 (NIV)
"You yourselves are our letter, written on our hearts, known and read by everyone. You show that you are a letter from Christ, the result of our ministry, written not with ink but with the Spirit of the living God, not on tablets of stone but on tablets of human hearts. Such confidence we have through Christ before God. Not that we are competent in ourselves to claim anything for ourselves, but our competence comes from God."

Everyone loves a good story, right? Where we sit on the edge of our seat...waiting to turn the page...what happens next? Oh, what a powerful moment in our lives when we stop and realize—we are living out that kind of story!

2 Corinthians Chapter 3 tells us we are like a letter written not with ink, but with His Spirit and not on a page, but on human hearts. What a beautiful description of our life in Christ. Doesn't it pour courage into your heart to know our stories are not only credible and authentic; but useful, powerful, relatable and true? Stories written with purpose and function in mind.

1 Corinthians tells us we are all part of one body with Christ as the head. Together we make a multi-functioning masterpiece. Not only are we gifted, but

we are equipped to live out our potential in Christ. For thousands of years we have heard stories, big and small, of those who use their giftedness in simple and humble ways and how the ripple effect never, ever ends. It all begins with the act of obedience.

What does the letter of your life look like? Are you fulfilling His plan for your story? Still seeking it out? That thought is sometimes scary, but when we break it down to steps we understand, the fear begins to fade away: 1) remember what you've learned; 2) pass on what you know; 3) ground everything in scripture; 4) let God do the work. The more we practice these steps, the more natural they become. The character and special strength that comes from Christ alone allows us the ability to live out the story, even when it's hard to see how a particular chapter might end. Don't give up, don't give in. Steady on, keep playing your part...a non-contributing member of the body means the whole body is suffering. We need you just the way God made you. Remember, your story is one for the ages. Don't change, alter or polish it...proclaim it! It's guaranteed to be a classic.

<u>Daily Focus</u>

Take a moment to write out your "elevator pitch" story (2-3 minutes). This is how your life was prior to meeting Jesus, how it changed and where you are now.

_____

_____

_____

_____

_____

_____

_____

_____

_____

_____

_____

_____

_____

_____

_____

_____

_____

Write a prayer today using the acronym **PRAY** below:

Praise -

_____

_____

Repent -

_____

_____

Ask -

_____

_____

Yield-

_____

_____

DAY 7: CELEBRATION
By Arra Murphy

*

Psalm 77:12 (NIV)
"I will consider all your works and meditate on all your mighty deeds."

Psalm 9:1 (NIV)
"I will give thanks to you Lord with all my heart; I will tell of all your wonderful deeds."

Do you ever feel like it is impossible to relate to God? You don't know the first thing about getting to know God or you don't feel worthy of His attention. I think everyone feels that way at some point in their life, maybe a few times. Circumstances can make you feel this way, face it we are all human and have made mistakes or have had doubts about God and his intentions.

Many things happen in life with no explanation, good and bad, but for some reason the bad is what seems to get most of our attention or occupy our minds. The bad makes us question our belief in a loving and caring God. Psalm 77:12 tells us to put it all out there, it gives us the permission to question and ponder our thoughts related to his intentions for our lives or our circumstances we are in. I tell you this out of experience not lightly to make a positive spin. We had a tragedy in my family many years ago. My cousin lost his 9 year old son to a brutal attack, it was unimaginable. His grief and the families grief was nothing I had ever experienced. I was a new believer in Christ and this opened up so many doubts about God. I questioned Him, got angry with Him and dare I say cursed Him. When I was completely broken and had no feeling left I went to the Bible and read scripture and began to realize that God allows things to happen in order to make His plan complete for us. It is shown time after time in the Bible for those who have unconditional faith. My cousin and his son were very close they were buddies. His son's swift death was in preparation for the father coming home to Jesus a year later due to cancer. You see it would have been extremely painful to watch his father's death and the father was much more at peace with what was going to happen to him knowing he would see his son in heaven and spend eternity with his son and God.

We are told to meditate on all of God's mighty deeds, why, so we look for answers, so we look at the countless things He has done for us and know that He is a loving father. The Bible is full of historical accounts of His love and blessings in good and bad circumstances, because His love is unconditional. God wants you to seek answers to your doubts because you will find them in the Bible. You will see His glory. He will reveal himself through scripture.

A natural consequence to this meditation is pointed out in Psalm 9:1 "which is giving thanks to the Lord with all your heart." Praise God every chance you get for His love and kindness, strength and wisdom and the blessings he gives you every day. Realize that He does bestow blessings on us constantly, don't take for granted the sunshine of the day or a gentle smile that you receive by a stranger. God doesn't have to prove his love for you in momentous ways they can be small things that mean a whole lot more. Don't miss them, say thank you! He has a hand in all that is right and good in our lives. When you truly realize this, you will praise Him unconditionally out of your faith and love. It will come naturally.

Make a conscious effort to get to know God, choose to know Him in faith. Read the Bible daily and you will be able to relate to Him. Praise Him for He is deserving!

Pray this today:
Lord your goodness and graciousness can be seen in a believer in Christ and will lead others to praise you. We give you the praise you deserve because you have proven your loyalty, your strength, your graciousness in so many ways throughout history and your eternal love for us through the sacrifice of Jesus Christ. You know our troubles Lord and you're bigger, you're caring love sustains us. Fill our hearts with your Holy Spirit that we may be a messenger of your love to others. Amen.

Daily Focus

In what areas of your life do you see God's blessings and unconditional love?

_____

_____

_____

Write a prayer today using the acronym **PRAY** below:

Praise- (List at least 3 things)

_____

_____

Repent -

_____

_____

Ask -

_____

_____

Yield-

_____

_____

WEEK 4:
RELATING TO THE WORLD

DAY 1: GOD'S WORD
Heidi Miller

✳

1 Timothy 4:6-10 (NIV)
"If you point these things out to your brothers and sisters, you will be a good minister of Christ Jesus, nourished on the truths of the faith and of the good teaching that you have followed. Have nothing to do with godless myths and old wives' tales; rather train yourself to be godly. For physical training is of some value, but godliness has value for all things, holding promise for both the present and life and the life to come. This is a trustworthy saying that deserves full acceptance. That is why we labor and strive, because we have put our hope in the living God, who is the Savior of all people, and especially of those who believe."

A few years ago I was challenged to ask my kids the question, "What is mama the most passionate about?" The question made me a little nervous. But the more I thought about it the more I started to see things in a positive light. That week we had spent time together as a family at home and sat together at church. I had been to the gym a few times that week and was trying to eat good food. Maybe, just maybe, they would mention those things. I got home that afternoon, gathered them in the living room and asked the question. My daughter Hayden's hand shot in the air and she had the biggest smile on her face. And then she said, "I know! Your phone!" My heart sank because I knew that in that moment she was a mini mirror of where my heart truly was. I had revealed to my kids what I valued by the way I spent my time. I had so hoped that the answer would have been Jesus or God's Word or at least my husband or family, but instead she answered with what seemed so obvious to her little eyes.

In the same way that my children were watching what I filled my heart with, the world is also watching. They need the hope of a living Savior, but unless we're filling our hearts with God's word and being nourished by His message, they will never see that in us.

Take time this week to turn everything off and focus on Him. Spend time in His Word and let it fill your heart. It takes time, work, and discipline, but it's so worth it! Whatever is truly in your heart will spill out when you speak, react and interact with those around you – and you never know who's watching!

Daily Focus

What would those closest to you say you're most passionate about? Does this reflect your love of Jesus?

Write a prayer today using the acronym **PRAY** below:

Praise -

_____

_____

Repent -

_____

_____

Ask -

_____

_____

Yield-

_____

_____

DAY 2: PRAYER
By Shannon Maupin

✱

Ephesians 6:18-20 (NIV)
"And pray in the Spirit on all occasions with all kinds of prayers and requests. With this in mind, be alert and always keep on praying for all the Lord's people. Pray also for me, that whenever I speak, words may be given me so that I will fearlessly make known the mystery of the gospel, for which I am an ambassador in chains. Pray that I may declare it fearlessly, as I should."

When I was a little girl, my mom taught me to pray before bedtime. We would fold our hands, bow our heads and recite together, "Now I lay me down to sleep, I pray the Lord my soul to keep…".
When I was in Jr. High, I took prayer to a new level. I liked this one cute boy, SO I started asking God every night to make that boy like me back. God, as a good father, said, "NO!" for my own good.

As an adult, I have learned to cling to prayer. I have prayed for my friends whose marriages were falling apart. I have prayed for my best friend as we watched her little girl take her last breath. I have prayed for my friends in other countries who could die for sharing their faith.

Prayer is more than just a few little cute lines or wishes for something we want. Prayer changes things.

God wants us to talk to Him ALL the time about everything. He never sleeps. He never goes out of town. He is never too busy to talk to us. SO we can always talk to Him about anything. We might not always feel like we are doing earth shattering things, but we can pray for the people who are. We get to partner with God when we pray for people who are declaring the Word of God.

Daily Focus

When you pray are you "Me-centric" or "Others-centric? How can you change this today?

_____

_____

_____

Write a prayer today using the acronym **PRAY** below:

Praise -

_____

_____

Repent -

_____

_____

Ask -

_____

_____

Yield-

_____

_____

DAY 3: SIN
Lori Murillo

*

Matthew 18:15-17 (NIV)
"If your brother or sister sins, go and point out their fault,
just between the two of you. If they listen to you, you have
won them over. But if they will not listen, take one or two
others along, so that every matter may be established by the
testimony of two or three witnesses. If they still refuse to
listen, tell it to the church; and if they refuse to listen even to
the church, treat them as you would a pagan or a tax
collector."

There is something about a sisterhood. A group of gals
you can call your people. You know the ones you call
in crisis, or in angst, or for a celebration. Funny
enough, I grew up without my people. For a long
while, I didn't have a group, and a group didn't have
me. Now whether or not this was a perceived reality
or a true reality is debatable. Nevertheless, early in life
I grew up feeling lonely. And forgotten. Left out.

In my 20's I found my people. While working for a
non-profit organization, a group of gals started a
vacation club – of mixed ages and personalities –
beginning adventures now lasting over 20 years.

When you walk through seasons of life without people
and then experience life with people, your
appreciation for belonging is profound. In reading and
reflecting on the passage, Jesus speaks of something

even MORE significant than that sometimes illusive sense of belonging. Healthy connections aren't solely based on 'feeling' connected. Jesus speak of our responsibility to our sisters in Christ. Relationally speaking, we have a "TRUTH IN LOVE" responsibility! Several words stand out in reading the text: SIN, GO (privately, then with others), FORBID. AGREE.

Could it be that we take our friendships too lightly? That when we see sin coming into play in our friend's life, we don't GO? That we let sin carry on because we avoid conflict? Consider that Jesus is telling us the truth is - FORBID sin, not only in our life (read Matthew 7:3-5), but also FORBID sin in our sisterhood. Is this true in your relationships?

Healthy relationships require truth. In this passage Jesus tells us healthy relationships also need AGREEMENT. While sometimes we avoid conflict, other times we spend too much time arguing, disagreeing with others' choices, rather than finding common ground. Could it be we give up and walk away too easily with our sisters? In this passage, the author teaches us to agree, to ask God, and to gather IN HIS NAME.

Healthy relationships require prayer. Beautifully, this relationship talk from Jesus contains a promise for dealing with sin and strongholds in our lives: verse 20, "...I am there among them." Twenty years later, amidst of highs and lows, my vacation girls would all agree He is among us. We are never alone when facing our sins and strongholds.

Let's be diligent today, inviting Jesus to bring truth-filled, sin-exposed, prayer-filled relationships with other sisters in Christ.

Daily Focus

Why do you think it is so difficult to not only accept truth from our "people" but also give it?

_____

_____

_____

Write a prayer today using the acronym **PRAY** below:

Praise -

_____

_____

Repent -

_____

_____

Ask -

_____

_____

Yield-

_____

_____

DAY 4: SERVING
By Erica Cox

*

1 Peter 4:10 (NIV)
"...use your God-given gifts to serve others."

Is service to God important to you? What does it mean to you? Service to God, in today's society, is certainly a countercultural concept. We are told to take what we want; take from others; and take from the world all we can. This idea is etched into our brains from an early age.

But God wants us to serve Him by serving others, rather than taking from them. How did God exemplify service to others as service to Him? God Himself modeled the most selfless act of love and giving to others. He gave us His only Son who died for us, so that we could have eternal life. God modeled unconditional love and service to all humanity. Can we do that? Can we live a life of service to God by serving others, and not expect anything in return? God has gifted and equipped each one of us to serve others in unique ways. 1 Peter 4:10 says it perfectly, "Use your God-given gifts to serve others." We live in a hurting and fallen world that needs people willing to go against the grain to give, not take.

But where to start? "Serving others" is a vague and broad construct. "Love begins at home," Mother

Teresa said. "And it is not how much we do, but how much love we put in that action."

Begin today by loving and serving your family. As a woman, wife and/or mother, we have the responsibility and the privilege, from God, to help direct our family to Christ Himself by modeling selfless service. It's easy to serve your family, but it must be done with joy and love. Love your family with all you have, speak kind words that bring life, do things without a complaining spirit, lay aside your agenda, sit and listen. Let's change the way we see serving, and see it through the eyes of our Almighty God as love in action.

Daily Focus

How can you serve someone today?

_____

_____

_____

Write a prayer today using the acronym **PRAY** below:

Praise -

_____

_____

Repent -

_____

_____

Ask -

_____

_____

Yield-

_____

_____

DAY 5: SACRIFICIAL GENEROSITY
By Joey Begley

✳

Proverbs 11:24-25 (NIV)
"One person gives freely, yet gains even more; another withholds unduly, but comes to poverty. A generous person will prosper; whoever refreshes others will be refreshed."

Is it really a "Dog eat Dog World?" Am I only required to "Look out for A, #1?" If this is true, it leads me to feel alone, lonely and depressed. Maybe there is something more. Perhaps the band, Three Dog Night, has it correct….just maybe "One Is the Loneliest Number." What if I got outside of myself and not only loved myself, but I loved others as well? What would that look like?

The Bible tells us in Acts 20:35, "It is more blessed to give than to receive." This is a hard concept to grasp. Try telling a three year old that it will give him joy to give away one of his toys…or even my ten year old for that matter.

Yet, I have found that God's economy works the opposite of what one might expect. In the place of giving this cannot be more true. The more you give, the more you receive.

Luke 6:38 (NIV)
"Give, and it will be given to you. A good measure, pressed down, shaken together and running over, will be poured into

your lap. For with the measure you see, it will be measured to you."

This truth doesn't make logical sense. I like to see things logically; this is hard for me to grasp, but I have personally seen it in my own life. You cannot out give God. Let's try not to put God in a box. He is God. He has every resource at his disposal. And quite frankly, He doesn't need our money. He wants you and me to experience the freedom and beauty in the art of surrender and giving. Once we surrender, the joy we experience cannot be matched.

Many people stop too quick in their thinking. It is tempting to give so that you will receive. And, it is tempting to think it stops right there. Instead we should think of it as this wonderful cycle. When we give, we are given more so that we can give more. When we talk about giving, our mind automatically jumps to the financial side of giving. And, yes, "giving" often has much to do with the giving of our resources, but it doesn't stop there and shouldn't stop there. We can also give of ourselves. We can give love, encouragement, grace, mercy, time, effort, a helping hand...even a smile. I believe it is true that you get back what you give out.

The Bible says "He who refreshes others will himself be refreshed." Proverbs. 11:25b. Try going an entire day being purposeful about refreshing others and see for yourself the joy that settles and rests in your heart. Try volunteering at an organization, serving food to the homeless, playing with children at a children's home, or talking with women at a pregnancy center. Then, ask yourself, "Who is being blessed here?" I think you will be surprised to find that the blessings are received on both ends… not only the one receiving the help, but, even more so, the one extending himself to love others.

Daily Focus

Do you currently experience the joy of God by being sacrificially generous? If not, what holds you back from taking this step of faith? Pray about that today.

Write a prayer today using the acronym **PRAY** below:

Praise -

_____

_____

Repent -

_____

_____

Ask -

_____

_____

Yield-

_____

_____

DAY 6: TELLING YOUR STORY
By Lucinda Hamilton

✳

Romans 10:13-15 (NIV)
"For everyone who calls on the name of the Lord will be
saved". How, then, can they call on the one they have not
believed in? And how can they believe in the one of whom
they have not heard? And how can they hear without
someone preaching to them? And how can anyone preach
unless they are sent? As it is written: "How beautiful are the
feet of those who bring good news!"[b]

I grew up in small town Oklahoma and was so very lucky to have grandparents that were the hands and feet of Jesus. They lived their lives based on this verse. My grandfather loved sharing the good news of God's forgiveness. He would tell anyone that would listen; that no matter what your guilt is, what your past was, whoever calls upon the name of the Lord will be saved! He was one of those people that would invite everyone and anyone to church. I remember having to get ready for church in the early morning hours just so we could have enough time to make our rounds and chauffeur all the neighborhood children that needed rides to church. Many of my friends were brought to Jesus because of my grandparents. He believed that if we reached these children they would lead their parents to Jesus. He was relentless in his duties given to him by God and he reached the masses. Because of his faith and the faith he instilled in my mother; I was raised knowing we are the beautiful feet that bring the good news of forgiveness. He died before I started working for Compass Church, but I know he is dancing in heaven knowing where my faith he taught me about has led me.

As the scripture says "how can they hear without someone preaching to them? And how can anyone preach unless they are sent?" God wants us to reach out to someone who needs him, but how can they call on his name and be saved unless we are willing to follow this request. We all have the most beautiful feet that can share the Greatest News there is! "God forgives every sinner who trusts in Jesus as their Lord and Savior! Let's tell everyone! OR as my grandfather would say "Shout it from the mountain tops"! Well there are no mountains in Oklahoma, but his shouts were heard across the plains of Oklahoma!

Let this be your prayer today.
"Father God, we know you want to send us to someone that needs you, I'll go to whoever you want to send me so I spread your good news….."

Daily Focus

List 2 people that you can share your story with this week?

1. _____
2. _____

Write a prayer today using the acronym **PRAY** below:

Praise -

_____

_____

Repent -

_____

_____

Ask -

_____

_____

Yield-

_____

_____

DAY 7: CELEBRATION
Written by Lisa Levine

✳

Hebrews 10:23-25 (NIV)
"Let us hold unswervingly to the hope we profess, for he who promised is faithful. And let us consider how we may spur one another on toward love and good deeds, not giving up meeting today, as some are in the habit of doing, but encouraging one another – and all the more as you see the Day approaching."

I struggle to follow the truth in this passage sometimes. Since we can trust God's promises, it is now up to us to help each other. But, I don't know about you, but it can be hard when balancing family, work and your marriage to make time to gather with like-minded individuals. This passage reminds that sometimes we need to accept those invitations to meet together with other women, as it can serve our hearts and spirit. As women we need to be nurtured and not just be the one nurturing. We need to encourage and be encouraged by other woman of God. If you make time for your heart and your spirit then you will be more open to God's presence and Word. Hold on tight to your faith and if you find it slipping away then find others to help you hold on. Life can be challenging sometimes, but God did not design us to deal with our circumstances alone. Let us all be encouraged by one another.

Jolly Rutten said, "A beautiful woman uses her lips for Truth, her voice for Kindness, her ears for Compassion, her hands for Charity and her heart for Love. For those who do not like her, she uses Prayer."

Daily Focus

Do you share your circumstances and challenges with other women? If not, pray today for God to lead you to women who can encourage and surround you with prayer.

Write a prayer today using the acronym **PRAY** below:

Praise -

_____

_____

Repent -

_____

_____

Ask -

_____

_____

Yield -

_____

_____

Made in the USA
Columbia, SC
26 April 2018